D0757926

CHARLOTTE FLAIR:
BOW TO YOUR QUEEN

TEDDY BORTH

abdopublishing.com

Published by Abdo Zoom, a division of ABDO, P.O. Box 398166, Minneapolis, Minnesota 55439. Copyright © 2018 by Abdo Consulting Group, Inc. International copyrights reserved in all countries. No part of this book may be reproduced in any form without written permission from the publisher.

Printed in the United States of America, North Mankato, Minnesota.
092017
012018

THIS BOOK CONTAINS
RECYCLED MATERIALS

Photo Credits: AP Images, Depositphotos Enterprise, Getty Images, iStock,
    Newscom, Seth Poppel/Yearbook Library, Shutterstock,
    ©Miguel Discart CC BY-SA 2.0 p. 18
Production Contributors: Kenny Abdo, Jennie Forsberg, Grace Hansen
Design Contributors: Dorothy Toth, Neil Klinepier

Publisher's Cataloging-in-Publication Data

Names: Borth, Teddy, author.
Title: Charlotte Flair: bow to your queen / by Teddy Borth.
Other titles: Bow to your queen
Description: Minneapolis, Minnesota: Abdo Zoom, 2018. | Series: Wrestling
    biographies | Includes online resource and index.
Identifiers: LCCN 2017939285 | ISBN 9781532121074 (lib.bdg.)
    ISBN 9781532122194 (ebook) | ISBN 9781532122750 (Read-to-Me ebook)
Subjects: LCSH: Flair, Charlotte (Ashley Elizabeth Fliehr), d1986- --Juvenile
    literature. | Wrestlers—Juvenile literature. | Biography--Juvenile literature.
Classification: DDC 796.812 [B]--dc23
LC record available at https://lccn.loc.gov/2017939285

TABLE OF CONTENTS

Charlotte Flair was born Ashley Elizabeth Fliehr on April 5, 1986. She was born in Charlotte, North Carolina.

Her dad is two-time WWE **Hall of Famer** Ric Flair. When Charlotte was 13, she helped her dad win a **match** by interfering in it!

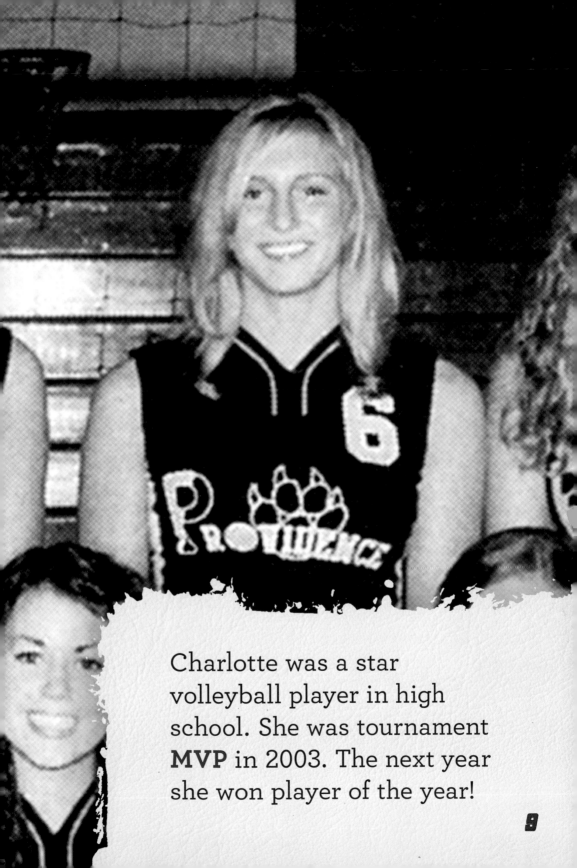

Charlotte was a star volleyball player in high school. She was tournament **MVP** in 2003. The next year she won player of the year!

In 2012, she decided to be a
wrestler like her dad. She had
never wrestled before. The WWE
took a chance on her anyway.

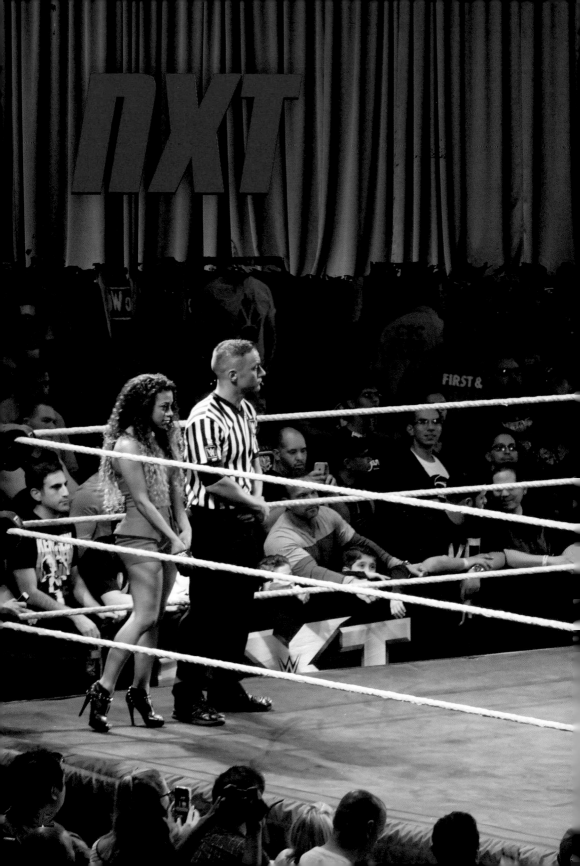

On July 17, 2013, Charlotte made her **debut** in NXT. WWE uses NXT as a place for wrestlers to grow and learn.

In less than a year, she was NXT Women's Champion. Charlotte's **matches** in NXT would help start **WWE's women's revolution.**

15

Charlotte made her WWE TV **debut** on July 13, 2015. Two months later, she won the Diva Championship. She would be the last to win it.

At **Wrestlemania** 32, the Diva **division** was changed to the Women division. Charlotte had a triple threat **match** with Sasha Banks and Becky Lynch for the new title.

Charlotte won! She became the first Women's Champion in the new **division**.

GLOSSARY

debut – to appear for the first time.

division – WWE has a men's division, women's division, and a cruiserweight division (for male wrestlers under 205 pounds).

Hall of Fame – an award given to an individual for a lifetime of work.

match - a competition in which wrestlers fight against each other.

MVP – stands for "Most Valuable Player" and is given to the best player.

Wrestlemania – WWE's biggest event of the year.

WWE's women's revolution – a movement in WWE to take women's wrestling more seriously by putting focus on in-ring matches and being more athletic.

ONLINE RESOURCES

Booklinks
NONFICTION NETWORK
FREE! ONLINE NONFICTION RESOURCES

To learn more about Charlotte Flair, please visit **abdobooklinks.com**. These links are routinely monitored and updated to provide the most current information available.

INDEX